Made of Glass

Carol Sheppard

Made of Glass

Carol Sheppard

Red Balcony Press

Made of Glass

First published in 2025
by **Red Balcony Press**

Red Balcony Press is an imprint of,
Black Eyes Publishing UK
Gloucester UK
GL1 3ET

www.blackeyespublishinguk.co.uk

ISBN: 978-1-913195-41-0

A CIP catalogue record for this title is available from the British Library.

Edited by: Josephine & Peter Lay

Cover: Jason Conway, The Daydream Academy
www.thedaydreamacademy.com

Every time I look at the night sky
I think of stars dying

Every time I look at the night sky
I think of stars dying

Contents

Who am I?

I am green meadows and brown furrowed fields
I am steaming black and white cows
in the milking parlour whose grey tongues
reach for you from under wet spotted noses.

I am the comfort of a real wood fire
spitting and glowing in the grate, with logs
axe-split by hand and stacked under the lean to
and dried ready for cold winter nights.
I am roast beef dinners, rhubarb crumble on a Sunday,
my mum always in the kitchen,
hands covered in flour,
the smell of pies and cakes baking in the oven
or cooling on the side.

I am a farmhouse miles from anywhere
where skies are as huge as the conker tree in the lane,
stars so bright they scorch your eyeballs
and devilish bats fly and dart for insects
in the farmyard at night.
I am where picnics in the cornfield
are summer days and Dad stops the tractor
to join us for a cool drink
and my sister and I climb stacks of piled straw bales.
I am braces of pheasants hung in the larder
cut down in their prime by the hay mower
plucked by hand on the doorstep, oven bound.

I am the roar of tractors,
I am the squall of sparrows in the hedgerows,

the call of cattle in the lower field,
the hawk that soars the sky.

My body is made from mud and grass and trees
I am the countryside and the countryside is me.

Copious

Copious is a trawler 13.9m in length built in 1999 and sails from Mevagissey, the second busiest commercial fishing port in Cornwall.

The *Copious* is late tonight
somewhere ten miles out.
Forecast: wind north westerly
sea moderate, harbour bound.

Tethered row boats quietly wait
bow to wharf in salt cracked harbour,
agitating water with rubber-tyred hulls;
lamp posts stand with dimmed glow.

Colourful houses on the curve of the hill
stretch windows towards restless waters,
lighthouse soberly watches, blinks safety;
the sea has nothing to say.

Out there, fortune is fish
every piece of gold must be taken
for every feast there is famine
net every shoal until heavy laden

Galaxies smear darkening skies
tide smacks against open harbour walls
out further deep waters chant grief's song,
restless winds rasp at the moon.

A shape on the horizon, steams forward,
bulk of black and white slides into harbour's
open arms, trundles between
roped vessels, bumps quietly to a halt.

Sword

He sleeps next to me
mouthing a scimitar smile
morning's gilded light splices curtains
rests like a sabre across his bare chest
the fuller cuts my neck first

Made of Glass

Glass delusion is a psychiatric condition where people believe themselves to be made of glass

Don't touch me!

I might shatter at any moment, splinter
into a million disco ball pieces of shrapnel
that crunch under feet, embed themselves in skin,
burrow into epidermis, into blood vessels,
float along with plasma, platelets, white cells
that sparkle in sunlight like CDs hanging over
a vegetable patch to keep the crows and pigeons away.
Can you see into my vitrine with your spy glass eyes
see my heart beating like bird wings, see my decanter lungs
fill and release, an hour-glass counting each breath
sand filling one lobe to another; my mouth,
my bocca, see how flames rise on my tongue, singe my lips
my rose window eyes full of stained glass
how the light catches bright to dark etching prisms
of colour stretch across mote filled spaces that sing into
empty rooms
There is no window to my soul - I'm made of glass.
You can see right through me.
I am fulgurite, fused by lightning, my transparency
my strength and my weakness unless I turn into mirror,
reflect what you yourself see
I live in fragile fear of cracking; I might even cut myself
on parts of me, shards of sharp glass, diamond blades
I stay locked in this prison, so nobody can touch me
so I don't smash into dust.

If the nightingale sings too high, its pitch shrill in the sky
my glass might creak and crack.

If a plane flies too low, its low rumble might shake me
like a tumbler swaying on edge of shelf.
The wind might blow me over, make me fall to the floor
or I could turn into a glass dragonfly, take to the breeze
float over looking-glass ponds
and I won't be afraid, my glitter wings strong
no fear of falling

But for now, please don't touch me
I'm made of glass

I might shatter.

Second Best

Do you know what it's like
to always be second best?
Like the antique grandfather clock
which stands by the door
chimes but not on the hour;
elegant but unnecessary -
like the Ercol table with a jagged scratch
covered by a tablecloth,
natural beauty stifled, hidden.

To be second best is like
tugging on a sleeve
trying to say you have been good
because you have been good
but not good enough;
like the doll with the broken leg
discarded at the bottom of the toy chest,
the kitten with the blind eye still at the shelter
broken and forgotten.

Being second best is a plastic shopping bag
rolling and blowing in the wind
but nobody runs to catch it,
like an unmade bed,
a withered bunch of flowers,
a used stamp,
a half-read book,
a blurred photo,
a disturbed lie in.

Is the moon second best to the sun?

The moon isn't always full
sometimes it's just a silver sliver
or covered in a blanket of grey cloud,
but does that mean it's not perfect,
that it cannot shine?
It shines whether it can be seen or not,
still lights dark places,
still pulls the tide to shore.

Quiet Man

At the end of the day
take me to my quiet man
the one with the busy mind
and few words.

Watch his eyes flare
when I arrive home
his smile, the way his eyes crinkle
and later, when I'm snuggled on the sofa
reading my book
he places a cup of tea by my side
and my favourite biscuit.

We don't always talk
but when his arms reach out
and he pulls me close
his heart speaks to mine
louder than any words could ever do.

Kintsugi

I read an article
about kintsugi
and when I saw you
broken
on the floor
I wanted
to join you
back together
with gold
to make you
more beautiful than before.

Next Door Neighbour

I knew it was you as soon as I heard the
shrill whine of the lawnmower I bet you're wearing
that stupid green padded jacket the one
that looks as if it belonged to your mother and she died
two years ago and I never liked her either with her
twitching curtains and raised eyebrows keeping a
watchful eye on everything and everyone
and you are just like her poking you nose into
conversations mowing the grass at eight am on a
Sunday and parking your car in front of my driveway
and I didn't say anything at first not as
your mother had just died and I felt sorry for you
but then you kept doing it and that noisy wooden
windchime that one that hangs in your tree and keeps me
awake all night when its stormy and I dream of
cutting the strings with scissors letting each bamboo
tube fall to the ground and I was pleased when
my cat shat in your garden and dug up your newly
planted onion sets and yes it was me that kicked your
kitchen waste bin down the drive and the lid
broke off and I should have felt guilty but I didn't
not after you blocked me in and went to the shop
to get your stupid magazine probably about trains
or toys or something and I was late for work again I
scratched your car with my key when you left it parked
across my drive again and there was no
neighbourhood watch or your mother to see it.

Journey

If we become separated, I
will wait for you
by the railway track, in case
you choose to follow
the rusted rails, jumping
from one blackened sleeper
to another as you go.

I will dispense dry leaves
to fly like moths to find you, send
a smoke signal from a dirty diesel engine
to mix with the peppermint clouds, startle
flocks of resting rooks hunkered in the trees
so they take flight, scatter like splashed ink.

I will sail flotillas of paper boats down the rivers,
light blazing beacons across the hilltops,
release bunches of colourful plump balloons,
fly flags from tall masts
and shoot fireworks into the night sky.

So that wherever you are
you will see that you are not alone
and know that I am close.

This poem was chosen and featured in the Of Earth and Sky project with artist Luke Jerram in 2020 and lines from this poem were painted on the ground and displayed in Gloucester.

Previously published in The Trawler 2020

The Shed at the Bottom of the Garden

There's an old shed
at the bottom of the garden
with a corrugated tin roof
boarded up sides
and a door that hangs listlessly
creaking like old bones in the wind.
They say a homeless man
used to live there
who couldn't bear to stay in a house
being a war veteran.
During the day he would drink cheap cider
swear at passersby in the lane
cough and spit into the grass
and at night he would shake his fist
at the moon, swear at God and Jesus.
He was known as Old Jack
always wore a khaki green overcoat
come summer come winter
given to him by the widow at no 32
used to belong to her long dead husband
who worked in insurance.
Old Jack is no longer there
his roll up lungs
and swollen liver have taken him
and the shed is now empty
covered in brambles and ivy.
A robin makes a nest there
every year hidden from view
beneath glossy leaves.

The rippled tin roof is rusty
coming away at the edges
the strong wind pulls at it.
Sometimes when I lie in bed
I hear it howl
like a wounded animal.

Your Lips

I hardly know you
don't know if I like you
or you like me
but I can only think of
your lips
I watch how they
curve and curl round words
how they rise at the corners
in a smile
I want to feel those lips on mine
feel them pressing on my neck
a kiss on my collarbone
a whisper on the flesh of my breast
those lips fill my days
my dreams at night
I don't understand why I
think of your lips constantly
when I don't even know if I like you
or you, me.

These Hands

These hands bent like dragon claws
are old and worn and tired;
blue rivers run through translucent land
between swollen knuckle hills.

These hands have cradled small babies,
rocked them to sleep, washed them clean,
wiped tears from sad soft faces.
These hands have held other hands,
felt safe and warm and loved,
tickled children, comforted friends.
These hands have fed chickens and lambs,
carried heaving buckets of water,
broken ice on farmyard troughs
so cows and sheep could drink.
These hands have hoed, pulled weeds,
planted seeds and raised vegetables.
These hands have kneaded bread,
baked cakes, cooked thousands of meals.

These gentle hands have caught spiders,
placed them carefully outside.
They have felt the warmth of log fires,
the coldest frosted mornings.
These hands have knitted and darned and mended,
painted, cleaned and scrubbed.

These hands bent like dragon claws
are old and worn but tender.
They've spent a lifetime holding onto love
keeping it clasped safely in their palms.

Wild Bathing

Fetch me a bathtub
and place it in a field
with an amazing view,
a hillside overlooking a wooded valley.
I can fade into lush green
with sunshine ragwort swaying,
white clover speckled grassy banks
stone walls zig zagging patchwork fields.

Fill that bath with warm water
bubbles right up to my chin
I could stay til dusk
gazing and dreaming and not thinking
birds could drop, fly away with my thoughts
And being alone would feel so good
I would wash it all over my body
drape myself in warm silence.

And I wouldn't even mind
if I had to sit at the end with the taps.

Dead Things

I'd always been fascinated by dead things
skulls, fossils, pinned butterflies under glass
so when dad came back from his walk
told me that he'd seen a giant sheep skull
I wanted it.

I don't know why I wanted it, I just did
a strange fascination with bones
of a creature now passed on.
I begged him to remember where he'd seen it.

That evening as the daylight fell to rose gold
we parked in the layby and climbed
over the stile built into the dry stone wall
placing feet on stone, on stone,
over, on stone then jump to ground.

We skulked like burglars into that field
although no crime had been committed
hunched our shoulders and made ourselves small
as we followed the curving wall through the
knee high rye grass, keeping to
a thin silver snail trail through the green.

We searched by torchlight until the skull was found;
it lay there in the fold between wall and ground
the rest of its body missing.

as I picked it up, a barn owl called
and bats flew like clouds of midges.
The skull was huge, bleached and moon-like

thick ring-marked curly horns spun
out in spirals for battle.

They left you like a beggar in the field
dead and worthless to the farmer's purse.
You must have been a magnificent beast.
to wear a crown like this.

Sheringham

We sit in tub chairs behind the glass of the patio doors
staring out as the sea turns silver and the peach sky pales.

Passing the binoculars between us we keep watch for invading ships. Observing the white sails of a yacht slide from left to right. Then spotting a low-lying container ship on the horizon in front of the wind turbines, fading into the evening haze. People-watching – the woman with the fat waddling pug, the couple with matching green fleeces, the three lads passing a cigarette between them. Our vision becomes obscured by midges with their ballerina moves and dangling tails dancing in front of the window. Rising and dropping in time to the tick of the clock.

Landslide

The rains came
The rains came again last night
The rains came again last night and washed the land
The rains came again last night and washed the land away
And my neighbours' houses too

The hillside slipped and the road cracked
A river of mud washed the land away
And the houses and the cars and all the trees
It washed all the trees away
It washed my neighbour's wife away

I stand here as the rains come down
I have no home
The rains came down again last night
Washed it all away

Skating the River

When Old Man Winter visited the valley
he'd freeze rivers, wide flooded meadows.
We'd brush cobwebs away,
unhitch our skates that hung like bats
from rusty nails in the basement,
make for the fields.

As morning sun burned through clouds
night heron roosted for the day
all the village kids swarmed
to skate on frozen rivers,
those flooded meadows
a swirling sea of colour,
woollen hats, thick woven coats,
knitted gloves, laughter.

How we loved to skate when ice
covered the land we knew
where we walked in summer
picnicked in the flowery meadows
fished for trout in shallow streams
to feel free in this contained world.

The crackle of frost in the air,
our streams of dragon's breath
as we held hands and skated miles of river
weaving across the glassy meanders
round the oxbow lake
where bullrushes and reeds stood
like soldiers frozen in time.

We'd stay until darkness folded
over the meadow
and the night heron broke the low horizon;
Reluctantly we'd return home
hoping the river would not melt
while we slept.

Previously published in Black Bough Winter Anthology 2024 as 'Night Heron'

Crossbones Girl

Cross Bones in Southwark, London is a pauper's graveyard referred to in a 1598 survey as a burial ground for 'single women', commonly interpreted as a euphemism for the prostitutes who worked in the surrounding brothels.

I was one of the Crossbones girls
scarred with pox and inhumanity
no ring on my wedding finger

Each night I stalked London's streets
alert, seductive, a ribbon at my slender neck
my mane of hair, my renowned beauty

I wore heels, fishnets, corsets of silver and gold
painted scarlet lips, charcoaled eyes, cheeks of rouge
wore a coat of mink on a hoarfrost night

Gentlemen could not resist me
paid a pretty penny
the glimpse of my pale skin made them weak

They would follow me, while I played them
plied my trade amongst the rich and famous
took the generous ones home

So they could gorge on me while I thought
of another life that had not been mine
I fed them scraps, the lies and compliments they wanted

When their time was up, I pushed them out
washed them from my body, straightened the bed
counted the notes left on the lace clothed table

Then I would put on my pure white nightdress,
neck to toes and brush my silken strands
sleep dreaming of the day

I walk through those iron gates
to be reunited the rest of the outcast dead
and find my little boy.

Fading Around the Edges

We were watching tv one afternoon
when I saw her staring at the plant in the corner;
my new acquisition from the garden centre.
Broad, rounded leaves, dark centre bleeding
to pale, red-veined rims
a beautiful variegated rubber plant.

I'm that plant. she said
What do you mean? I asked, edging closer
That's me, she said, *I'm fading round the edges, losing my colour*
Don't be silly. I said.

I was afraid now this plant might shrivel
and die like the others.

I fetched my daughter a glass of water
and opened the curtains just a little bit wider
to let in more afternoon sun.

Anglerfish

When male and female anglerfish mate, they melt into each other and share bodies forever. The deep sea is so vast that if a male finds a female he latches on and fuses to her, losing his eyes and internal organs until the two fish share a bloodstream.

I wake to voices floating across the harbour:
clank of chains, soft chug of boats;
know before I open my eyes, you are gone.

I miss the way you held me in your arms
last night, your soft kisses on my skin,
how we melded together and it felt right.
We clung to each other as anemones

cling to rocks, begging the moon not to rise,
the tide not to turn. Melted into each other,
danced as high flung herring quiver
silver in moonlight.

How we lost our eyes, became blind,
our limbs and muscles merged,
your skin became my skin,
our blood shared the same veins.

Now in morning's wide yawn,
the screech of the black headed gull
cries from my own strangled throat.
My hand reaches and feels the chill

of the empty sheet, your scent drifts
away like a schooner chasing the waves.
I knew that the sea would call you back.
I miss you.

Symonds Yat to Portishead

A pair of pub garden benches were washed up on a beach almost 50 miles away, after being swept away by floodwater 19.11.2019

I smiled when I heard the picnic benches had turned up
carried downstream by the river's autumn storms;
watery arms dragging pine from grass bank to pebble beach.
Symonds Yat to Portishead.
Now they rest between lighthouse and city.

It made me remember that time in June -
we had sat at one of those picnic tables,
by the murmuring river, hands entwined,
carved our initials in a never-ending lover's heart
as the evening sun sank behind the horizon;
drank cider from pint glasses and you fed me titbits
from your plate when I wasn't hungry for food,
only ravenous for you.

And now, the news says the missing picnic tables
have been found – and just like you,
washed fifty miles downstream.
I like to think that you might see them there
on the beach and remember me
as I remember you, with love's first passion,
maybe recall the girl you left fifty miles upstream
that summer, when we drank cider from pint glasses
by the murmuring river as the sun sank behind the horizon.

And if you happen to walk along that beach
wonder if I sent that bench to you.

Drowning

We are both drowning in our own ways;
You, taken by the water,
me, by the absence of you.
Every day waves wash over me.

I can hardly picture your face.

The void you left within me screams.

The Birds

As soon as the words left his mouth
the cage door opened
ten thousand birds flew out
all cackling and calling to each other.

Their wings beat with such feroity
the earth shook, ground shifted
obsidian skies dripped black
as they spiralled in huge dark clouds.

For days they hung around there in the skies,
they perched in the silver birches outside her house
preening themselves on the telegraph wires.
At night, crowing with cruel throaty croaks.

Some stayed in the house and she had to shoo
them off the draining board as she washed the dishes,
others emerged when she opened cupboards.
They sat on chairs when she tried to watch tv.

Some crept up the counterpane at night
to give a nasty nip when her eyes were closed.
They rested on her pillow, whispered in her ear
and when she slept, they flew into her dreams.

Their constant cawing tormented her
every day, every night they followed her,
to the bus stop, the corner shop, even to put the bins out.
Thousands of them, every time she stepped outside.

No sunlight could get through, plants withered and died,
the air heavy, she could scarcely breathe without wheezing
their fallen feathers spread across the carpet and tiles.
They pecked, clawed her skin until bruised, scarred.

The bitter tang of their guano in the house
splattered on the rugs, the windowsills,
made her mouth sting, eyes water.
However much she washed, the stench would not go.

After many weeks she got used to the birds being there,
tried to ignore their beady eyes watching, heads sideways
their constant presence in the house, on chairs, tables,
on top of the kitchen cupboards, on her headboard at night.

Her skin grew so tough from relentless pecks and scratches,
began to grow stubble which changed to feathers.
Her face grew thin and her nose curved towards her mouth.
Her eyes grew round, black and beady.

As she lifted her hollow boned arms
the birds around her cocked their heads,
squawked high pitched cries, flapped at glass.
She opened the kitchen window and all the birds flew out.

She took a last look around, stretched her own wings
and followed the flock over dark tree tops.

Feathering the Nest

He sits on the dining room chair
awaiting the cut from my inexperienced hands.
I level blades at his neck, cut a straight line
through hair that curls at his collar
then pick up the comb, run it through silky
white strands using its teeth as my guide.

Soft, white hair falls to the floor in clumps,
we joke about birds finding a soft lining for their nests.
I follow the shape, his rounded head, cutting carefully,
the balding top now liver spotted, where single hairs
sprout as weeds in barren ground. I snip them one
by one, a gardener taming a forgotten garden.

Then ears, follow the curve of the lobe,
the spikes in the folds and on the ridge.
Sideburns, stiff like brush bristles snap and crack
as the stainless-steel blades come together.
Then eyebrows. He frowns, clenches his brows together
I say close your eyes and keep still. He does.

I take the wild wiry brow hairs between my fingers
cutting gently, keeping pointed scissors away from eyes.
He sighs, my voice an echo in the distance
as his hearing aids wait patiently on the sideboard.
Next a stray hair or two on his nose, fishing rods
thrown out to sea. He trusts me.

All finished, I brush white down from his shoulders.
He stands, puts the chair away. Then we fold the sheet,
corner to corner, over and over, into the middle

so that the snowy fuzz stays incarcerated in the cotton panel.
We spy a stray lock and joke we'll be in trouble with mum
as she's already hoovered that morning.

He takes the sheet outside and lets the wind waft his hair;
the birds can feather their nests with it, if they want to.

Previously published by Atrium Poetry, April 2024

And what if there was no sunset

no slow turn of light;
no drip, drip of sallowness - blue to orange
to pink to shimmering silver,
when the day drifts into murk and
falls, down, down deep into darkness?

And what if there was a snap, a switch
and the light went off and it was black, just …black?
No in between - just light and dark, day and night,
perfect view to nothingness
where you couldn't see your hand in front of your face.

And when the sun was gone birds would fall from the sky,
creatures would scamper underground,
claws scrabbling to safety of burrows.
Wolves would wake and howl when the moon
showed its precious slice of gold
and stars would switch gleam like fireflies in couch grass
quivering and bleaching in the shadows.

And would the beasts and black cloaks
steal from the woods, from under rocks towards our homes,
surrounded by screeching bats, clouds of flapping moths?
And those people who were late …too late,
would they find their way home
with no light to guide them?

I mean, would I find my way home?

Ice Breaker

at the office party pre-covid

"Aren't ice breaker ships fascinating?"
I said as the crowd dispersed,
us two, bobbing buoys tethered
by politeness to the ocean floor.
"Do you know they have special engines
and curved bows to break the ice,
can sail the harshest seas.
The toughest ships in the world
smashing through the thickest ice fields;
frozen plains shattering under pressure."

His eyes skimmed the room, looking
to the horizon, searching out
a beacon of saviour light.

"Did you know they have reinforced hulls,
are coated in friction-reducing resin,
wider at the front and rounded to ride the flows."
The way he looked at me, eyes narrowed,
sharp as those ships' angular prows;
I ploughed on headfirst, my course set,
straight for the midnight sun.
Breathless at the ships' super strength.

He stared at me, unable to grasp the
wonder of vast frozen seas being broken.
Asked if I wanted another drink.

Postcard

with a nod to William Carlos Williams

I'm sorry
I went
without you.

You said
you didn't
want to go.

I think
you would
have loved it
here.

Previously published in Beat Surreal 2025 by Gloomy for Pleasure.

Previously published in The Trawler 2022

Angel

All Hallows Eve, just after eleven;
I'm in the bus stop when I see her coming up the road;
an angel in white, perfect, pure. . . walking slow,
talking with a witch. She must have fallen,
her knee is cut, heels scuffed, laddered tights.
She carries a bottle of vodka, taken from some poor soul,
to rescue them from the dreaded drink.

She staggers, stumbles, the worries of the world
too much for her thin frame, narrow shoulders,
then curls over clutching her gut,
pain too much, vomits in a shop doorway,
sickened by the sins of everyone here.
She must have been crying, her lips all smeared,
cheeks streaked with black run tears.

She's joined by a vampire and a zombie in a puffer jacket;
unafraid, she hugs them both and slips her arm
through the zombie's, calls them friends, holds them dear.
She shivers, her sheer dress no match for this weather.
The zombie offers his coat, she shakes her head,
takes the cigarette from the vampire's mouth,
puffs once then throws the glowing stub onto the wet
pavement; another pair of lungs saved.

She must be an angel, her white fluffy wings and silver halo
glittering under the orange glow of the street lamp.
She is just too beautiful for this ugly world.

The Only Star in my Sky

Dusk brought a blush to an ink-stained sky,
highlighting the end of summer.

No clouds nor moon but you stood out,
a glowing beacon, a lone figure in the night;
radiating light and strength, piercing my dark.

You were there when I needed you,
that night.
I should have listened to advice;
now I'm here, the evening creeping round my shoulders.
wondering if you were a sign, my destiny.

You called to me in a soft whisper,
entranced me with your eyes, seduced me
with your smile, your touch, your scent.
I didn't even notice if there were other stars,
your light shone so bright.

My mother wouldn't have liked you
but I was drawn to you, had eyes for no other;
I was lost too soon, in a fiery dream.
I felt your strength that night;
you gave me purpose, a path to follow.

I couldn't reach you, of course,
your distance too great, your fire too hot.
You were already dying, burning out like a meteorite
before your time, and mine.

I would have followed you to the end
...if you'd have let me.

I blamed the moon

when the wildness struck;
spinning away on my own axis
to the far side of the moon.
The gravitational pull was too strong,
tides pushed and pulled me,
surged blood along my veins.
I circled the earth in waves of light,
my dark side hidden from view.
Later, I waned, when the neap tide came
and the sun died for the day.
I shouted and screamed and danced at the moon
but there was no reply.

I told everyone the moon made me do it.
Said it was just a phase I was going through.

Sunrise to Sunset

I used to love the way he spoke to me … his words wafted
like waves washing pebbles on a shingle beach, they ebbed
and flowed, soft and gentle, singing me a lullaby.
And I, childlike, listened to the rise and fall of his voice;
new and exhilarating, I never tired of hearing him talk.
His breath close to my cheek, caressed my warm skin.
He dipped into my bare soul and found life and love there.
His lips would find mine, then kissing me,
he'd whisper my name, like a badge of honour.

I lie next to him in our stiff white marital bed,
hear his deep breaths stifle the room; him relaxed,
unaware, snoring like a full fed cat, plump and purring,
oblivious to the vast icy gap between us, a deep
incurable fissure where winter's chill enveloped
our cosy home, snuffed out the warmth, the fire.
Where his words grate and rasp against every nerve
and bone in my body.

I like the sound of his snoring, relish the peace
before he wakes; before his harsh voice
and cruel words break the morning in two.

Little Bird

I am that little bird
that sits silently outside your window
in the old twisted fruit tree
camouflaged behind rotting pears
hanging corpses who failed
to let go and fall in Autumn

I am that little bird
with the soft brown feathers
sharp beak, sharp claws
who watches bright eyed, protective,
waiting patiently for the wind to change

I am that little bird
who builds her nest with sticks and grass
hidden away on high branches
which sway precariously in the breeze
fiercely defends her eggs and young

I am that little bird
that sits silently outside your window
you don't notice me there, do you?
until I start to sing.

Cake

Today I will bake a cake like my mother used to;
in the aga warmed kitchen, cat cosy, views of the flower
filled garden, apron clad and humming.
Cakes; more than just mouthfuls of soft sponge:
tastes of home, coal fires, warm hugs.
I will measure with care - butter, flour, sugar and fruit,
a good pinch of cinnamon, not too much salt.
Mix well but do not over stir.
I'll place the cake carefully in the oven, middle shelf,
turn once, watch the time ticking so it doesn't burn.
Place gently on a wire tray to cool.
I will present the cake to my mother, even though
she may not recognise me.
Maybe the smell will bring her home …

#

Barista

We wait in line behind the couple
in matching raincoats, outwardly patient,
inwardly seething, itching to look at the time
Minutes tick past. Fresh barista coffee takes
so long despite vast numbers of staff; only one
working the immense metallic coffee machine.
Tubes hiss and spit water, frothing milk
into jugs. Dark fragrant liquid splits,
drains into pure white coffee cups
and the smell of strong coffee rides the breeze.

We sit at the table in the corner
Surface sticky, sugar splattered,
She drinks hers black and I pour milk,
add sugar and stir clockwise.
Her phone is already in her hand
Fingers and thumbs flick rapidly.
I try to make conversation, talk about
the weather, her day at work.
But she's not listening, engrossed in her online world.
I repeat my question and she slides her eyes to meet mine
I can almost hear the tut in her mouth as she speaks
"Why do you want to know?"

Barefoot on Hidden Lawns

Always restless,
she walks barefoot onto hidden lawns
leaving tiny footprints in the pillow snow;
perches upon splintered fence,
behind ice coated bird bath,
pulling green puffer jacket tight
around her sparrow frame.
Like a bird in winter,
eyes always skyward, keen.
Weak winter sun emerges
bright against milky clouds.
She pulls back her head, closes her eyes,
stretches arms wide as if in flight.

A flock of raucous rooks fly over.
I watch her flutter and know
that any time soon she will join them.

Summer of 1976

We climbed the five-bar gate, made a nest in the corn
spread the woollen blanket on the gasping ground
cracks wide enough to put our hands in
we told stories and jokes, my sister and I
giggled at spotted ladybirds waddling up corn stalks
lay, watched flocks of sparrows blot the sky
two buzzards patrolled the high thermals
soaring, two as one, perfect harmony
we stayed until our stomachs called us home
sun dipping behind trees in the spinney
us wading through waves of flowing corn
we argued on the way home, my sister and I
on who should carry the dusty blanket
while aeroplane trails split the evening sky.

Mermaid

That night, I found a mermaid
at the bottom of my third pink gin
amongst lumped ice and juniper berries
lazily swimming on her back, circling the glass bowl.

She grabbed my hands and dragged me under.
We swam, our bodies, skin to scales.
She took my face in her hands,
kissed me hard;
Chilled salt lips, so soft;
her hair, ribbons of seaweed, caressed me,
tail wrapped tightly round my legs.
She pulled back, laughed at my expression,
sea-green eyes searched mine,
brows arched,
flicked her shimmering tail.

She wanted to take me deeper,
to where light fades to darkness,
to a trench where night creatures prowl
and sea cucumbers writhe under jellyfish glow.
I imagined spider crabs with gigantic stone legs,
toxic breathing tube worms,
viperfish with sharp spiny teeth and deadly
frilled sharks, jostling and fighting in the gloom
around rusty barnacled wrecks.

I gasped, struggled for surface;
gulped great lungfuls of sweet air.

When I turned around
she was gone

the sting
of her kiss
still on my lips.

Grey Lag Geese

Germany 1942

Each night we were woken,
dragged from feather beds
to hide under hedges,
lie in damp ditches,
listen for engines' hiss
as grey metal birds
flew over us like the flocks
of grey-lag geese who came
each summer to our meadows,
migrated in Autumn;
wedges of silver arrows.
English planes came seeking
skeins of giveaway lights,
clutching fragile eggs.
We would roost there all night
awaiting morning's chorus
so we could go back
to our downy nests to sleep.

Mistle Thrush

They say we are the harbingers of the storms,
that we beckon inclement weather
and we laugh like whores.
They call us Mizzly Dicks and Jeremy Joy
because they are afraid of us.
We speak with seven tongues and not as deaf
as they believe.
They say we are mystical because we do not feel
the cold, happy to sit in frozen treetops,
play our flautists clarion
to call the forests to war.
They call us the devourer of mistletoe,
don't understand how we stomach the poison
of the pale green berries
when they believe it will cure their ills.
They call us Big Mavis and Bull Thrush because we are the
commanders of the tree tops, fly with a rhythmic
beat to our white flash wings.
They call us Shrike and Jercock when we call to each other
in broken tones, sing loud in squalls of snow.
They call us Masters of the Coppice
as we hunt and forage our forty acres.

They say we are the harbingers of the storms.

'Highly Commended'
Gloucestershire Poetry Society 2024 Open Poetry Competition.
Subsequently published in OPC2024A

Sparrows

It's the same time every morning.
You could set your watch by them -
- the flock of brown house sparrows
that cluster in the goat willow
outside my window
bringing a noisy version of their
choral assembly and my morning
to life.

Swans

Inspiration for this poem came from watching a video about an injured swan who had been in a rescue centre for three weeks and was brought back and released. Her life long mate was delighted to see her.

My bones rattle marrow-empty,
heartstrings sliced from an echoing chamber of vaulted ribs.
Even the sun can't puncture my dejected skin as I circle
the stagnant lake, dark and deep, neither ripple nor splash.
One solitary swan paddles, head hung as a withered bloom;
twenty-one missing heartbeats.
White coats bring a feathered angel,
patched wings wrapped in green canvas.

Released, she slides to her soulmate.
Like a mirror's image they rise and fall,
creating shapes in a lover's concerto,
where harps and cellos strum pain away.
Dipping and nuzzling, two halves as one,
forming the perfect heart, then
pirouetting, twirling, breathless.

Then I catch your reflection in the water
as you glide into view,
the light behind you a heavenly glow.
My emptiness becomes filled with the sounds
of an almighty choir singing arias
and I become whole again.

Potato

How easily the knife slips under fleshy skin
revealing white undersides
skin speckled with liver spots.
it reminds me of you. Of you at the end
when, at last, you had been felled;
the mighty oak of the family.
Your hand gripped mine,
tissue paper skin, bruised blue.

For the first time ever, I heard
you utter *I'm scared*
I couldn't look at your face,
studied your hand instead,
counting spots like dying stars.
You'll be ok, I whispered back,
my fingers clasped round yours.

But I was afraid too.

Athena

Pass me my spear and my shield
the one with the gorgon's head,
strap my breastplate across my chest
over my favourite dress
the one which flows like the sea
on a blustery day;
then take me to the front line
before my dumb ass brother
lurches forward with his
bloodthirsty sword and tiny mind,
before he takes all the men of Olympus
to their godly deaths in chariots of gold and fire.

Let me be that voice of reason,
the thought before action;
let me shine like the sun
over the Parthenon in battle,
let my woman's strength be stronger
than all the armies before me.
Keep my people safe in these treacherous times.

Take me away to:

a little smuggling village by the sea
where squat whitewashed cottages line winding lanes
and hidden alleyways; where cow parsley
and buttercups splash colour under leafy hedgerows
and the wind on the cliffs blows your liver out
from between your ribs, to the falsetto of a herring gull.

Take me there in a car loaded with buckets and spades,
smelling of lemon sherbet. With sun hats
and a tartan blanket obscuring the back window
and the radio playing Top 40 tunes

and I'll be wearing my shorts and strawberry print tee-shirt,
sunglasses on and the wind in my hair
as we sail the rough seas of the motorway.

Sophie and Emma will be on the back seat
singing along to the radio.
I'll catch their eye in the mirror,
Sophie will scowl and Emma will laugh.

We'll park the car, link arms and head down hill,
stopping for a cream tea on the way.
Eat a scone as large as a house, until we feel sick.
Later, we'll head for the beach, strip to our swimsuits
dive into the waves. Swim towards the horizon
not knowing if we will ever turn back.

November in Portland

Growling November winds snicker
around my ankles, barbed spikes
penetrate goose-pimpled skin.
Exposed on this jagged outcrop
facing to restless seas where
waves snap and snarl as they ravage
sharp sand and slick pebbles;
crescent moon beach curving
as your warm body once
curled around me.

Dare I step out of this Jurassic rock
cut from chert, hauled from under
tough turf sprinkled with vetch, trefoil,
where stones lie peppered
with lichen and liverworts?

Do I reveal my true self, my other half
or remain in limestone shadow -
one rock amongst thousands?

Pike

Esox Lucius

Jealousy

                                        is a pike
resting in sleepy shallows
amongst twisted reeds, gnarled roots
ever vigilant in gloomy shadows,
elongated green speckled body
camouflaged, fins tickling the surface.

It will curl and spring without warning.
There is no way back.
It will catch you in its mouth
                                        swallow you whole.

You need to fish carefully -
Sit with patience and time;
and on a grey day,
catch him on your hook;
He will fight hard, twisting
and retching, spinning the line.

Bring him in close, scoop up your net,
stare face to face at this fragile creature
                                        then let him go.

Apple

I saw a discarded apple on the pavement.
It reminded me of you;
withered and bruised,
not the rosy beauty you once were.
Teeth marks on your skin, a chunk missing,
open wound to the core.

I should have picked you up,
placed you somewhere safe.
But I walked away
and let some other git kick you in the gutter.

Previously published in The Trawler 2021

I Asked the Wind

I asked the wind where he'd come from?

He told me where the pines touched the sky
and the grey squirrels roam the trees.
Chased clouds along the winding river Wye,
where salmon run,
past old stone bridges and closed down mines.
He told me that he'd made
the River Severn rough and angry,
made the waves rise and fall violently,
tossed boats and yachts like sticks.
The seagulls tried to outrace him
but even they could never catch him.

I asked the wind what he was going to do now?

Spend some time here, he mused.
blow gently across brown and green patchwork fields,
make the golden barley and wheat shudder,
bend the tree tops and watch the rabbits play.
Race up the hills and sprint for the skies
then dive bomb to the valleys below.
Make children wonder as the wind blows their hair
and makes balloons and kites fly.
See buzzards waiting on the wing
and swallows dip and soar.

I asked the wind where he was going?

He said he was going across the county
across villages, the ploughed fields, church steeples

then on to Symonds Yat Rock,
where deer wander the bracken covered paths.
To see the sun and rain light a rainbow,
before moving on over dense dark forests
where boars roam and the tall trees grow
and no man lives for miles.
He'd visit the farms and blow seeds
across roads which cut through the countryside.
Watch horses canter and shake their manes,
speed the length of rivers and ripple the lakes,
follow the trails of wild animals
and miles of railway track stretched like threads.

I asked the wind what he would do then?

Then, he said, he'd rest awhile where the two rivers
meet and the skies are clear and cloudless.

The Severn Serpent

i.

rumours started again when a man's body
was found early morning on the riverbank,
legs splayed in a rat run of mud
where the body had been dragged
towards the water line, trousers frayed,
seams torn, legs bloody and scratched,
his neck twisted. Snapped.
Then two black and white cows found at the water's edge,
caught in branches of a tangled willow tree,
legs skywards, bodies rotund, bloated, grey tongues
dangling from stiff hollow mouths,
strands of grass blades still at the corners.
Farmers crops failed, people fell ill with flu,
took to their beds and the vicar
fled his parish without due notice.

ii.

villagers began to talk about the river serpent
returning; memories of long dead grandparents
spilling out stories, recollections of them huddled
around smoky coal fires, tales
of a monstrous black scaled creature
who lived in the depths, rose out of the water
to bring plague to the people, spoil farmers' crops,
devour children and cattle in its monstrous jaws,
the sound of crunching bones and skulls
resounding across marshland.

iii.

whispers started when the strange tides came
in Spring, carried huge walls of water
up the estuary swirling like a maelstrom,
gulping and spitting. They said it meant the serpent
was restless, waking from its slumber
some eight fathoms deep;
it's huge tail spooling and spiralling silt into watery clouds;
cows were moved to higher ground, broken fences repaired,
sheep became skittish, ran wild-eyed to shelter
in their stone-walled folds and the hens stopped laying.

iv.

during daylight hours the river seemed calm, serene;
sailed smoothly between flower-meadowed banks
where trees trailed leafy fingers in the scurrying flow.
Moorhens and swans floated and grazed
amongst the crested iris and woodland phlox,
blackbirds and sparrows fluttered in hedgerows
filled with delicate dog roses and spiky blackthorn,
but at night the black oily surface growled and hissed,
rose and fell, ripples circled with dangerous rip tides.
Old wooden boat hulks lay dead, rotting hulls sunken
in bottomless mudflats under the dark skeletal shadows
of the bridge, their tar blackened timbers arched
like a ribcage of a decayed and discarded whale carcass.

v.

local men started night watches, collected driftwood,
fallen branches which burnt bright beacons
along the river banks. Crumpled mole skins and dead crows
hung like ghoulish bunting on taut barbed wire
stretched from fence post to fence post.

A curfew was imposed; no one allowed out after dark;
women and children lay huddled in their beds,
blankets drawn up to their eyes, scarcely comforted
by the glow of lamplight in their windows to scare
the scaly serpent, keep it from their hearths.
Meanwhile, the men hunched over crackling fires
under star lit skies, ever watchful, afraid they might hear
the clack of its mighty jaws and torrent of gushing water
as it rises out of blackened depths.

vi.

months passed, men grew weary of long sleepless nights,
children forgot about the watery monster,
played outside once more,
women's talk turned to local gossip; their laughter rang out
across the village green, as the church bells chimed.
If the river serpent was close, no one knew;
the night watch was abandoned, the curfew lifted.
A new vicar came with hope and prayers in his leather case.
Fields grew green and crops ripened,
cattle and sheep grazed peacefully
and the hens started laying again.

Acknowledgements

A big thank you to Josephine and Peter Lay for publishing my first collection under Red Balcony Press (Black Eyes Publishing UK) and their assistance with editing and preparation of this manuscript.

To Jason Conway of The Daydream Academy for the brilliant cover design.

Also, to Karlostheunhappy and Ivor Daniel for all their help and support, for talking poetry for hours and our trips out to interesting places.

To Dean Writers Circle and Gloucestershire Poetry Society who have encouraged me as a writer and to share my poetry with others.

And to all those poets and writers who struggle daily with the difficult task of writing, you all inspire me.

Carol Sheppard

Carol Sheppard doesn't know whether to write poetry or plays so writes both. Her poetry story began when she was 10 years ago and wrote a 15-stanza poem on George and the Dragon while her classmates were struggling to write four lines.

She has been published in several poetry journals and anthologies and her poems have been exhibited in the Biggar Poetry Garden and Poetry Posts in Bream and Portland, Oregan.

She was thrilled to be Poet in Residence at the Gloucestershire Poetry Festival 2023. She is an active member of Gloucestershire Poetry Society and Dean Writers Circle.

Full Quotes

Carol Sheppard's debut collection glitters with reflections on life, love and longing, but Nature is the ever-present backdrop in these imagistic poems. From the initial poem, 'Who am I?' we see how the poet has been formed by her natural environment: 'I am the squall of sparrows in the hedgerows… I am the countryside…' Carol's ability to place us is masterly and her voice clear as she leads us into each poem with confidence. Birds swoop and fly throughout this collection; the sea is a recurrent theme as are fields and the wind. In the poem 'Mistle Thrush' she uses myth to perfection; 'They say we are the harbingers of the storm.' In other poems, her strong narrative style hints at Carol's additional talent, playwriting; her characterisation is strong and the tenderness with which she portrays her loved ones, heartwarming. The reader is captured, drawn through this collection, delighted at each turn of subject and yet over all is the feeling that life and reality are fragile; as though Made of Glass.
Josephine Lay, Poet & Writer, author of 'A Quietus' & 'Creating Stanley' (novel)

"A deeply engaging collection of poems that take in a breathless range of people, places, emotions, events, history, myth, landscape and nature. Some read as last love letters to a disappearing countryside, others reflect on the minutiae of love, passion and the everyday domestic details of shared lives. A poetry collection that you will reread again and again."
Dr Jason Griffiths senior research fellow University of Gloucestershire & co-director Reading the Forest

Carol Sheppard delivers a menagerie of stanzas made of glass; fragile and universal right from the leading epigraph, to the magnificent 'Copious', and across white paper skies of cynicism and humour. Songs, often ornithological, of aging and mortality, histories, nostalgia and longing, as in the William Carlos Williams'-inspired 'Postcard'. Settle down with an insightful survey of people and places with this debut collection, a fitting first foray for Red Balcony Press. –
Karlostheunhappy
2022-2023 International Beat Poet Laureate (England)

'These are colourful, relatable, keenly-observed poems by a talented writer. I particularly enjoyed the more descriptive and emotional poems from imagistic, painterly pieces on horizons with distant boats and turbines to a field with a lone animal skull that is a crown of its own body. The intriguing reflections on identity and musings on love make this an appealing collection for a wider audience.'
Matthew M C Smith, author of The Keeper of Aeons

In Made of Glass, Carol's debut collection, we are given generous and personal poems about desire, longing, love, loss, revenge, the ways we might heal 'the broken pieces.' And we are given the countryside, so important to the poet. Not simply as a place of beauty – 'green meadows and brown furrowed fields' – but as a place where a sheep's skull can be found 'the rest of its body missing'. As readers we are shown how our encounters, with the sea, the river, the land, build our identities. Throughout there is a sense of time passing, of mortality, the complexities, challenges and fullness of lives. It's a book about vulnerability, as in the poem, 'Made of Glass.' And transformation – 'I am that little bird.'
Belinda Rimmer, Poet

www.ingramcontent.com/pod-product-compliance
Ingram Content Group UK Ltd.
Pitfield, Milton Keynes, MK11 3LW, UK
UKHW021816160825
461930UK00007B/102

9 781913 195410